W9-DHI-825

GOLD RUSH!

BY ELIZABETH KRYCH AND ILLUSTRATED BY STEVE JAMES

SCHOLASTIC INC.
New York   Toronto   London   Auckland
Sydney   Mexico City   New Delhi   Hong Kong

For my Golden State family–E. K.

Many thanks to the special collections librarians
at the New York Public Library.

Page 3, page 5 (left) © J. Helgason/Shutterstock; Page 5 (right) © goldenangel/
Shutterstock; Page 8 © Jim McMahon; Page 9 © DreamWorks/Photofest;
Page 10 © Duncan Walker/iStockphoto; Page 14 © ullstein bild/The Granger
Collection, New York; Page 16 © Minnesota Historical Society/CORBIS; Page 17
(bottom) © AP Photo/file

No part of this publication may be reproduced, stored in a retrieval
system, or transmitted in any form or by any means, electronic, mechanical,
photocopying, recording, or otherwise, without permission of the publisher. For
information regarding permission, write to Scholastic Inc.,
Attention: Permissions Department, 557 Broadway, New York, NY 10012.

ISBN 978-0-545-35551-3

Copyright © 2011 by Scholastic Inc. All rights reserved.
Published by Scholastic Inc. SCHOLASTIC and associated logos are
trademarks and/or registered trademarks of Scholastic Inc.

12 11 10 9 8 7 6 5 4 3 2 1   11 12 13 14 15 16/0

Printed in China 68

Designed by Jennifer Rinaldi
First printing, October 2011

Table of Contents

A GOLDEN SURPRISE AT SUTTER'S MILL

The greatest gold discovery in history happened by accident.

Before the Gold Rush, few people lived in northern California. Claimed by faraway Spain, and then by Mexico, the land was sparsely settled by Native Americans, farmers from America and Europe, and Spanish-speaking cattle ranchers called Californios.

In the 1830s, a Swiss man named Johann Sutter obtained a large piece of California land from the Mexican governor. He had big plans for his land. Sutter hired workers to build a sawmill along the American River, which would be used to cut up pine trees for lumber to build a settlement.

But Sutter's plans took an unexpected turn. One of the workers building the sawmill on January 24, 1848, was a man named James Marshall. As he worked, he happened to see a glint in the riverbed. He reached in and pulled out a yellow pebble, then a few more. "Boys, I believe I have found gold," he told the other workers in wonder.

That night, he and Sutter performed tests on the golden material to make sure it was really a precious metal and not fool's gold. (So many people have confused a mineral called **pyrite** with gold that it is commonly known as "fool's gold.")

But Marshall and Sutter had not been fooled—the pebbles were real, pure gold. The workers on Sutter's property gave up the lumber plan and instead started looking for more gold.

What is gold?

GOLD IS AN **ELEMENT**, a naturally occurring pure substance. It can't be broken down into other materials. Gold's rareness makes it valuable. Throughout history, gold has been used to symbolize people and events that are special: Royal crowns, Olympic medals, and wedding rings are often made of gold.

GOLD

PYRITE

GOLD TERRITORY

Just a few days after Marshall's gold discovery, California became a territory of the United States. (A **territory** is an area directly controlled by the federal government, without the structure of a state.) But no one in Washington, D.C., knew that the new territory held great riches in its soil.

News of the gold find spread slowly. Four months after the discovery at Sutter's mill, in May 1848, rumors of the find finally reached San Francisco, a town 130 miles away. One day, an excited merchant named Sam Brannan held up a clear bottle full of gold pieces in the town square, shouting "Gold! Gold from the American River!"

Within days of seeing this proof, nearly everyone in the town hurried to the gold fields. They closed up their shops and left their jobs, taking all the shovels and pans they could find. Farmers left their fields and cattle, and sailors and soldiers left their ships and forts.

By August 1848, acting governor Colonel Richard Mason estimated that about 4,000 people were **prospecting** in the gold fields. Some scraped the gold out of cracks in rocks with their hunting knives. One man was said to have stubbed his toe on a golden boulder. Others found **nuggets** the size of baseballs mixed in the gravel of streambeds. Many dredged up amazing amounts of gold by **panning** in rivers, or passing gravel and dirt through strainers.

STAKING A CLAIM IN 1848

Because California was a territory of the U.S. and not a state in 1848, it was unclear what the laws were. It seemed like the land belonged to no one, or to everyone alike. There were no police or taxes, and the gold-crazy prospectors weren't too concerned about following rules, anyway. To keep some sort of order, each prospector chose a piece of land as his own private digging ground by filing a declaration of ownership called a **claim**. The size of a claim was limited to the amount of land that one man could work on his own.

While the claim system seemed fair to the prospectors, it ignored the Native Americans and Californio ranchers who already occupied the territory. As Johann Sutter feared, even though he had claimed the land of the first gold discovery, he was unable to keep prospectors from just helping themselves to his

Gold Country

Sacramento ★

San Francisco

CALIFORNIA

Los Angeles

San Diego

The California Mother Lode

THE **MOTHER LODE** WAS the main track of gold found in California. It stretched 120 miles in a thin strip north to south. Loose pieces of gold formed deep in the earth were slowly lifted to the surface by the motion of rivers.

crops, his trees, and his cattle. He didn't make a fortune; in fact, he lost most of his land.

In the summer of 1848, gold was relatively plentiful and could often be found close to the surface. The area of discovery was big enough that people could spread out and stake claims far apart from one another. California's governor confidently wrote, "for the present, there is room enough for all."

El Dorado found at last?

IN THE 1500s, IMAGINATIVE Spanish explorers thought the golden clothes of the Muisca tribe in South America came from an entire city made of gold. They called this city El Dorado, meaning "the golden one." During the Gold Rush, California was sometimes referred to as

Spanish explorers searched the Americas for an imaginary city of gold.

El Dorado, because it seemed like the "lost treasure" of the Americas had been found at last.

Today, there are several towns in California named El Dorado, as well as Eldorado National Forest, near where gold was first discovered. El Dorado County contains the land of Sutter's original holding.

EXTRA! EXTRA! GOLD BY THE BUSHEL!

There were no telephones in those days, or even a telegraph line across America. The fastest way news could travel a far distance was by ship. It still took several months for word of the California gold to reach Asia, Australia, South America, and the big cities of Europe and the eastern United States.

The rumors seemed too good to be true, but doubts were put to rest in early December, when President James Polk confirmed the discovery and put samples of California gold on display in Washington, D.C.

With that assurance, many Americans were seized by "gold fever" or "gold mania." Soon it seemed everyone was talking about the amazing wealth to be found out West. On remote farms and in bustling cities, people decided to try their luck in California. The thousands of people who made their way west beginning in early 1849 called themselves forty-niners.

When California became a state, this bear flag was adopted. Many forty-niners stayed and became California citizens.

Most of the forty-niners were young men with the means to pay for their trip. They came from a variety of backgrounds across the entire United States: farmers, factory workers, store clerks, blacksmiths, even ministers and lawmakers.

Worth your weight in gold?

THE AVERAGE PRICE OF gold in 2010 was approximately $1,250 per ounce. That's just over $20,000 per pound! To calculate the value of your body weight in gold, simply multiply your weight by $20,000.

For example, if you weigh 80 pounds, the value of your weight in gold is:

80 x $20,000 = $1,600,000

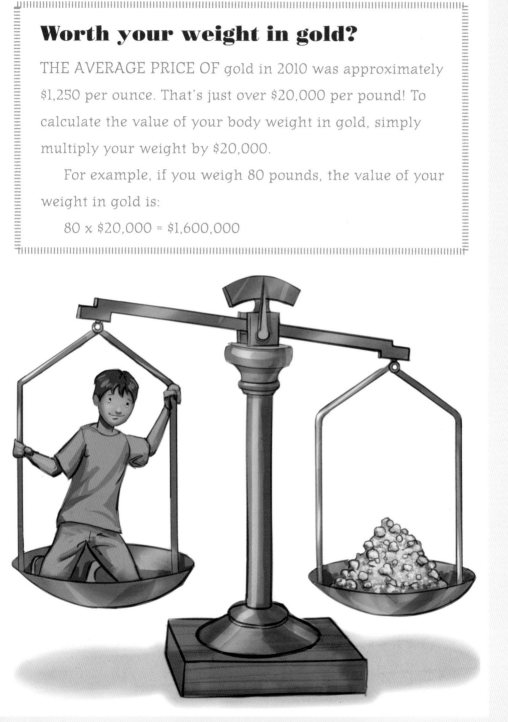

CALIFORNIA, HERE THEY COME!

Getting to California by land or sea in 1849 was a risky adventure. One inventor started selling tickets at $250 apiece for a flying machine that would take prospectors to California by air, but his invention never got off the ground. There was no way of avoiding it: The 2,000-mile or more journey was difficult and took many months.

Those who lived inland outfitted wagons with oxen and supplies. They started driving west once the weather was warm in the spring of 1849. The travelers were challenged by deserts, mountains, and rivers. Many of their animals wore out and died. Although the gold seekers brought rifles for protection against Native Americans, the real dangers on the trail were diseases.

Starting in Boston, New York, or New Orleans, the sea route went south all the way to the tip of South America and then north back up the west coast of the Americas. It took at least three to four months to make the journey, and often much longer.

like **cholera**. Despite their high hopes, many forty-niners died along the way west.

Forty-niners who lived close to ports went to California by ship. At first it was exciting to be on the open sea. Many had never been away from home before. But there were also many hardships on this route, from bad food and seasickness to the risks of disease and shipwreck. And after several weeks at sea, many voyagers regretfully wrote of being bored and homesick.

CALIFORNIA AT LAST!

After their long voyage, the forty-niners at last arrived in San Francisco Bay. Their first view was the eerie sight of hundreds of ships abandoned in the harbor. Everyone aboard had hurried to the gold fields—no sailors were left to sail the ships back home!

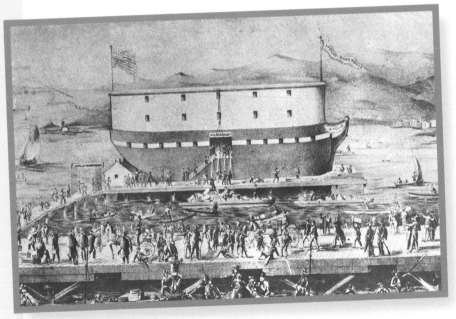

Some abandoned ships in San Francisco Harbor were dragged on land and used as stores, saloons, or hotels!

Forty-niners may have tried to bring all they would need with them in their wagons or luggage, but often most of their supplies were used up along the way or had to be left behind to lighten their loads. Some had brought fancy-looking "gold panning machines" from stores in the East that weren't of any use. What they really needed were simple tools, heavy-duty clothes, and food. One famous story tells of a man offering $10, a day's pay, for just one biscuit!

After buying tools, food, and a horse or mule, the forty-niners headed northeast by wagon or steamboat to Sacramento and the broad area of hills and rivers where most of the best claims were.

PROSPECTOR SHOPPING LIST

frying pan	coffee
coffeepot	pick
knife	ax
salted beef	shovel
salted bacon	mining pan
flour	tobacco
jerky	candles
dried fruit	pickles

OUTFITTING THE FORTY-NINERS

It's not a coincidence that Sam Brannan, the first person to announce the gold findings in San Francisco, was not a prospector. He was a store owner who later became a millionaire selling supplies to miners. The first miners wanted to keep their findings a secret so they could each gather up as much gold as possible. But merchants, ship owners, lawyers, and bankers wanted to stir up excitement and attract prospectors who would need their services.

From 1849 on, many people who came to California to dig for gold gave up their claims and went into business instead. Useful supplies were always in demand. One cargo ship arrived with a freight of ice, another with a hold full of rat-catching

cats. Anyone who could sell something the miners needed did well. Some people even assembled the frames of entire houses and floated them up the river to Sacramento. Others took supplies by mule team to set up shops in the camps.

General stores sold the food, clothing, and equipment that miners needed.

Forty-niner fashion

YOU MIGHT BE WEARING a hand-me-down from the Gold Rush right now! Did you know that blue jeans started out as pants for gold miners?

Levi Strauss was born in Germany and came to America as a teenager. When he heard about the California gold, he traveled west to open a shop in San Francisco. In 1870, Strauss and a partner, Jacob Davis, obtained a patent for heavy-duty pants made from denim cloth and reinforced with metal rivets. Strauss's company still exists today, as Levi's, and the jeans designed for gold miners are popular around the world.

The forty-niners needed tough clothes for the demanding outdoor work of prospecting.

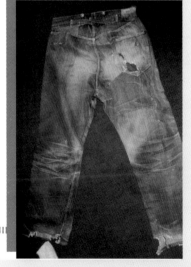

These early denim jeans from the 1870s are not that different from the popular pants many people wear today!

GETTING THE GOLD!

With a pick to chip rocks, a shovel to dig, and a large, shallow pan, a forty-niner could get started panning for gold as soon as he staked a claim. No matter how hard a miner worked, though, finding a rich strike was usually just pure luck.

Most of the gold was in tiny pieces, mixed in with rocks and dirt. Because gold is heavier than water and sand, it was simple to use water to separate gold flakes from dirt and mud. As time went on, miners began to dig even deeper, leaving the land cratered with so-called **coyote holes**.

All a prospector had to do was crouch in a stream, scoop a handful of river mud into his pan, and slosh around the water and dirt until the shiny gold collected at the bottom of the pan. This was called panning or washing the gold.

mining pan

cradle

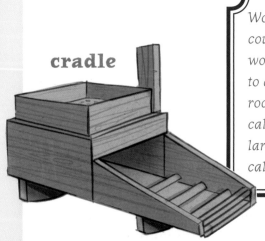

*Working with partners, a miner could process more gravel with a wooden box on rockers connected to a ridged chute. Because of its rocking motion, this device was called a **cradle** or a rocker. A larger version of the cradle was called a **Long Tom**.*

mining shaft

As surface gold became harder to find, deep mining shafts were dug, and steam engines were brought in to break rocks and dig tunnels. Big pounding machines called **stamp mills** broke up quartz rocks for the gold within.

stamp mill

Mining companies dammed rivers to get at the riverbeds. With big fire hoses, they used water to blast away at hillsides, a process called **hydraulic mining**.

hydraulic mining

LIFE IN THE CAMPS

Life in the mining camps was dirty, smelly, and rough. Forty-niners slept in tents or shacks, and the camps were dusty or muddy, and littered with trash. Most forty-niners let their hair and beards grow long; they weren't too careful about washing themselves or their clothes, either.

Except for the few who brought their wives along to help, the miners had to do their own cooking, laundry, and mending. Their food was limited to what they could hunt and what merchants brought in, and prices were very high. A lucky miner might average finding between $10 and $20 a day in gold at the most, but often they found nothing at all. One egg or potato could cost up to 50¢, and coffee was $4 a pound. Prices for tools, supplies, and animals were high as well. The forty-niners worked from

Forty-Niner Menu

Coffee
Hotcakes
Antelope steak*
Pork and beans
Biscuits**
Canned sardines
Whiskey
Dried apples

*If you can shoot an antelope
**Watch out for bugs!

dawn till dusk six days a week, but unless they were very lucky, it was hard to save up money to take home.

Around the campfire at night, the miners played fiddle, banjo, or guitar. They made up songs to cheer themselves up. One popular song, to the tune of "Oh, Susanna!" had this refrain:

Oh, California! That's the place for me!
I'm bound for San Francisco with my washboard on my knee.

Sometimes musicians and theater troupes passed through the camps and put on shows. Even bad singers always got lots of applause from the weary miners!

he names of the amps and towns that sprang p showed both the hope and ardship of life as a forty-niner.

GOLD IN ANY LANGUAGE

About 75 percent of the forty-niners were white American men, but the rest of the prospectors came from other places. It was often said that in the gold fields, all men were equal, no matter what their jobs had been back home. In California, everyone was equally crazy about gold!

After Marshall's discovery in 1848, some Native Americans began panning for gold, but as more whites moved in, many thousands were kicked out or killed by disease or violence.

News of the gold find reached Mexico and South America in the summer of 1848. Thousands of people who had mined for silver in Chile and Mexico hastened northward to try their luck with gold.

Some Europeans who wanted a new start set out on the long sea journey to California in 1849. Many Jewish merchants

from German-speaking areas of Europe became successful businessmen in California.

Not all miners came of their own free will. In the 1840s, slavery was legal in the American South, and a few slave owners brought their black slaves with them to help dig their claims. Sometimes a slave found enough gold, though, to buy his own freedom.

From travelers and letters, Chinese people heard stories of *Gum Shan*, a "golden mountain," across the Pacific. They wanted to get their own share of the gold! Unlike the English-speaking forty-niners, most of the Chinese immigrants were poor. They could not afford the cost of a ship ticket, so mining companies paid for their passage in exchange for free labor. By 1852, more than 20,000 Chinese had made the trip.

GOLD RUSH GALS

Less than 10 percent of the forty-niners were women, but those who did choose to go west had a unique adventure. Mining in the gold fields was hard and rough work—no job for a lady, it was thought, although some tried. A handful of women were seen dressed in trousers and "washing for gold" in the cold streams.

The women who did not prospect for gold made another kind of discovery, however. They found that in camps of only men, their skills were literally more valuable than gold! Women could do miners' laundry, cleaning, and cooking for good money. After seeing their success, men often gave up mining and went into business with their wives.

In the East, sometimes laws prevented women from owning property and earning their own money, but in California there were no such laws. One woman dressed as a man and drove a stagecoach for a living. Another made a fortune baking pies, while a third went into business as a portrait photographer. In the cities of San Francisco and Sacramento, women who owned hotels, restaurants, and theaters were prosperous citizens.

THE GOLDEN STATE IS BORN

Within just one year, 30,000 people from all over the world had settled in San Francisco, making it the most diverse city in America. Prospectors brought their languages, foods, religions, and customs with them. In their letters and diaries, forty-niners from the eastern United States conveyed the unique sight of Asians, South Americans, and Europeans all doing business together.

If a miner could afford luxuries, there were many places to spend his riches in San Francisco. Hotels and restaurants offered fine meals under crystal chandeliers. With gold in his pocket, a forty-niner could enjoy a hot bath, a play or concert, a night at the circus, gambling, billiards, and even bowling.

The well-to-do citizens of San Francisco were eager to have an official government, and the United States wanted to have more control over the gold-rich territory. On September 9, 1850, President Millard Fillmore granted statehood to California. The citizens of the new thirty-first state celebrated noisily in the streets when they learned the news from an arriving steamship.

GOING BUST

Seeing the Elephant

MINERS SUMMED UP ALL their fear, excitement, hardship, and disappointment in the expression "seeing the elephant." On the way to California, the elephant represented the adventure and unknown danger which the miners expected to find. But the idea was used to express failure, too, and it was said of forty-niners who gave up and went home that they had "seen the elephant's tracks" or "the elephant's tail," and had had all the adventure they could take!

By the end of 1849, 90,000 people had arrived to look for gold in California. None of the forty-niners became millionaires overnight, as they had hoped. While the first prospectors in the summer of 1848 had found gold fairly easily, by the time the forty-niners arrived the remaining gold was harder to get at. Many discouraged miners turned to crime. Prospectors now faced a new danger—that their claim would be stolen out from under them, a practice called **claim jumping**.

Disappointed and tired, forty-niners grew weary of the hard conditions of their work. They stood in cold streams all day, bending over to shovel dirt, enduring temperatures over 100°F in the summer. Many suffered from bashed fingers or broken bones. The rough camp conditions gave rise to disease, and most every miner dealt with bedbugs, fleas, and lice.

Tired and penniless, thousands of forty-niners were eventually forced to give up and go home. Some got stuck in San Francisco, trying to earn money for a ticket home, and stayed on to work in the city or start a farm nearby.

JOAQUIN MURRIETA WAS KNOWN as the fiercest bandit of the Gold Rush. A Mexican prospector, it was said that white settlers had jumped his claim and killed his family, driving him to seek revenge. He was depicted as a dashing, mustached Californio on a horse. His scary henchmen had names like Three-Fingered Jack. He may have been a real person, or a combination of different outlaws.

WANTED

JOAQUIN MURRIETA
For Murder and Robbery
JULY 1853

THE GOLD RUSH'S LEGACY

For all the riches that were found in California during the Gold Rush, much was lost, too. The miners killed or scared away most of the wildlife in the Mother Lode area. They dug deep holes, scraped away hillsides, and built dams, changing the course of waterways and disrupting farms.

Although much of the gold-rich area was taken over by large mining companies throughout the 1850s, a few prospectors hung on to their claims. About $10 million a year continued to be mined for a decade. Other major gold rushes happened later in the 1800s: the Black Hills rush, 1874–1877, in South Dakota

JANUARY 24, 1848
James Marshall finds gold in American River on Johann Sutter's land.

MAY 1848
Sam Brannan brings news of gold to San Francisco.

DECEMBER 8, 1848
President Polk officially announces the gold discovery and puts gold on display.

SEPTEMBER 9, 1850
California is made the 31st state by President Fillmore. The news reaches California on October 18.

JULY 1853
Infamous bandit Joaquin Murrieta captured by California State Rangers.

territory, and in the Yukon territory of Canada in 1898.

San Francisco remains to this day one of the most diverse cities in the world. The independence and optimism of the Gold Rush days live on in its reputation for tolerance, ingenuity, and individuality. In memory of that extraordinary time in its history, San Francisco's football team is called the 49ers. The nickname of California is the Golden State, and the state motto is a Greek word, *Eureka*, which means "I found it."

Not every forty-niner found gold, but they all discovered adventure.

APRIL 1849
First U.S. Post Office opens in San Francisco.

BY DECEMBER 1849
90,000 gold seekers have arrived in California.

1859
Discovery of silver in Comstock Lode, Nevada Territory.

OCTOBER 1861
Cross-country telegraph line completed.

MAY 1869
Intercontinental Railroad line completed.

GLOSSARY

cholera: a serious intestinal disease carried in polluted water.

claim: the area allowed for one person to dig for gold in.

claim jump: to take over another prospector's area.

coyote hole: a shallow hole dug and abandoned by prospectors.

cradle: a gold prospecting device made of a wooden box on rockers with a chute.

element: a pure, natural substance that can't be broken down into smaller parts.

hydraulic mining: a large-scale mining method using water power to blast away soil.

Long Tom: a large version of a cradle with a larger box and chute.

mother lode: the main underground location of a mineral. In California the **Mother Lode** of gold is about 120 hundred miles long and runs north to south in the Sierra Nevada mountains.

nugget: a golden pebble.

pan: to prospect for gold by swirling dirt and water in a shallow dish.

prospect: to search in the earth for natural resources.

stamp mill: a large machine for grinding gold out of raw quartz.

pyrite: an iron-sulfur mineral that is shiny like gold but lacks gold's other properties.

territory: land owned by the United States but not part of a state.